CONTENTS

- Program for string concatenation
- C program to Reverse a String using recursion
- C Program to arrange numbers in ascending order
- C Program to find largest element of an Array
- Sum of array elements using Recursion: Function calling itself
- Sum of array elements using pointers
- Program to find the size of an array
- C Program to Find the Largest of three numbers using Pointers
- C Program to Count Vowels and Consonants in a String using Pointer
- C Program to Print String using Pointer
- C Program to Swap two numbers using Pointers
- C program to create, initialize and access a pointer variable
- C program to calculate and print the value of nPr
- C program to calculate and print the value of nCr
- C Program to Multiply two Floating Point Numbers
- Program to multiply two numbers using function
- Program to find Quotient and Remainder
- C Program to find the Average of two numbers
- Program to find the average using function
- Calculation of mean by using Array
- Calculation of mean by using Array
- Counting Positive, Negative and Zero in an Array
- Program to convert binary to decimal
- Program to convert Decimal to Binary
- Program to convert decimal to octal
- Program to Convert Octal to Decimal
- Program to convert Binary to Octal
- Program to convert octal to binary
- Program to calculate Area and Circumference based on user input
- C Program to calculate Area of Equilatral triangle
- C Program to Print names of all Files present in a Directory
- Copying the contents of one file to another file
- Separating odd and even numbers in a file
- C Program to copy string using strcpy() Function
- C Program to copy string without strcpy() function
- How to use gets() function
- Switch Case with break

- Switch Case without break
- Program to check if input character is a vowel using Switch Case
- Basic do while Loop Program
- Swapping tow Numbers without using a Temporary Variable
- Program to find Sum of Digits of a Number
- Program to reverse a String
- Program to find Armstrong Number between 1 to 500
- Program to check whether a number is Armstrong Number
- Program to find exponential without using pow() method
- Program to insert an element in an Array
- Simple Program to remove Duplicate Element in an Array
- Program to check whether a two dimensional array is a Sparse Matrix
- Program to remove Duplicate Element in an Array
- Program to find Deteminant of 2x2 Matrix
- Calculation of Employee payroll using Structure
- Basic C Program for Pointer to a Pointer
- C Program to check lowercase using islower() Function
- Program to check uppercase using isupper() Function
- C Program to covert character to lowercase using tolower() Function
- C Program to convert character(s) to uppercase using the toupper() Function
- C Program to check if character is alphabet using isalpha() Function
- C Program to check if character is alphabet using isalpha() Function
- C Program to check if character string is alphanumeric using isalnum() Function
- C program to merge two files
- C program to delete a file
- C program to generate random numbers
- C program to print date
- C program to get IP address
- C program to shut down or turn off computer
- C program for Windows XP
- C program to merge two arrays
- C program to print Floyd's triangle
- C program to print Floyd's triangle using recursion

Displaying Hello World

```c
#include <stdio.h>
int main()
{
  printf("Hello World");
  return 0;
}
```

Calculation of Simple Interest and Compound Interest

```c
#include <stdio.h>
#include <conio.h>
#include <math.h>
void main()
 {
  float p,n,r,si,ci,t;
  clrscr();
 printf("Enter Principal amount :");
 scanf("%f",&p);
 printf("Enter number of years :");
 scanf("%f",&n);
 printf("Enter rate of interest :");
 scanf("%f",&r);
 si=p*n*r/100.0;
 t=1+r/100;
 t=pow(t,n);
 t=p*t;
 ci=t-p;
 printf("Simple interest = %10.2f\n",si);
 printf("Compound interest = %10.2f\n",ci);
 getch();
 }
```

C Program to check whether the given integer is positive or negative

```c
#include<stdio.h>
void main()
{
int num;

    printf("Enter a number: \n");
    scanf("%d",&num);
if(num >0)
        printf("%d is a positive number \n", num);
elseif(num <0)
        printf("%d is a negative number \n", num);
else
        printf("0 is neither positive nor negative");
}
```

Reverse a given number using Recursion

```c
#include<stdio.h>
int main()
{
int num,reverse_number;
  printf("\nEnter any number:");
  scanf("%d",&num);
  reverse_number=reverse_function(num);
  printf("\nAfter reverse the no is :%d",reverse_number);
return0;
}
int sum=0,rem;
reverse_function(int num){
if(num){
    rem=num%10;
    sum=sum*10+rem;
    reverse_function(num/10);
}
else
return sum;
return sum;
}
```

Program to find largest of three input numbers

```c
#include<stdio.h>
int main()
{
int num1,num2,num3;
    printf("\nEnter value of num1, num2 and num3:");
    scanf("%d %d %d",&num1,&num2,&num3);
if((num1>num2)&&(num1>num3))
    printf("\n Number1 is greatest");
elseif((num2>num3)&&(num2>num1))
    printf("\n Number2 is greatest");
else
    printf("\n Number3 is greatest");
return0;
}
```

Preparation of Student's Marklist

```c
#include <stdio.h>
#include <conio.h>
void main()
{
  char sname[30],course[30],sem[15];
  int cacc,bcom,cprg,clab,rdbms,tot;
  float perc;
  clrscr();
  printf("Enter the Student Name :");
  gets(sname);
  printf("Enter the Course Name :");
  gets(course);
  printf("Enter the Semester Number :");
  gets(sem);
  printf("Enter mark for VB:");
  scanf("%d",&cacc);
  printf("Enter mark for .NET :");
  scanf("%d",&bcom);
  printf("Enter mark for C++ Programming :");
  scanf("%d",&cprg);
  printf("Enter mark for C Practical :");
  scanf("%d",&clab);
  printf("Enter mark for RDBMS :");
  scanf("%d",&rdbms);
  tot=cacc+bcom+cprg+clab+rdbms;
  perc=tot/5.0;
```

```c
printf("Total = %d\n",tot);
printf("Percentage = %7.2f\n",perc);
getch();}
```

Fibonacci Series in C using loop

```c
#include<stdio.h>
int main()
{
int count, first_term =0, second_term =1, next_term, i;
    printf("Enter the number of terms:\n");
    scanf("%d",&count);
    printf("First %d terms of Fibonacci series:\n",count);
for( i =0; i < count ; i++)
{
if( i <=1)
      next_term = i;
else
{
      next_term = first_term + second_term;
      first_term = second_term;
      second_term = next_term;
}
    printf("%d\n",next_term);
}
return0;
}
```

Program to find factorial

```c
#include<stdio.h>
int find_factorial(int);
int main()
{
int num, fact;
   printf("\nEnter any integer number:");
   scanf("%d",&num);
  fact =find_factorial(num);
   printf("\nfactorial of %d is: %d",num, fact);
return0;
}
int find_factorial(int n)
{
if(n==0)
return(1);
return(n*find_factorial(n-1));
}
```

C Program to find prime numbers in a given range

```c
#include<stdio.h>
int main()
{
int num1, num2, flag_var, i, j;
    printf("Enter two range(input integer numbers only):");
    scanf("%d %d",&num1,&num2);
    printf("Prime numbers from %d and %d are:\n", num1, num2);
for(i=num1+1; i<num2;++i)
{
    flag_var=0;
for(j=2; j<=i/2;++j)
{
if(i%j==0)
{
        flag_var=1;
break;
}
}
if(flag_var==0)
        printf("%d\n",i);
}
return0;
}
```

C Program to check Armstrong number

```c
#include<stdio.h>
int main()
{
int num,copy_of_num,sum=0,rem;
   printf("\nEnter a number:");
   scanf("%d",&num);

   copy_of_num = num;

while(num !=0)
{
    rem = num %10;
    sum = sum +(rem*rem*rem);
    num = num /10;
}

if(copy_of_num == sum)
    printf("\n%d is an Armstrong Number",copy_of_num);
else
    printf("\n%d is not an Armstrong Number",copy_of_num);
return(0);
}
```

C Program to check if a number is palindrome or not

```c
#include<stdio.h>
int main()
{
int num, reverse_num=0, remainder,temp;
   printf("Enter an integer: ");
   scanf("%d",&num);
   temp=num;
while(temp!=0)
{
    remainder=temp%10;
    reverse_num=reverse_num*10+remainder;
    temp/=10;
}

if(reverse_num==num)
    printf("%d is a palindrome number",num);
else
    printf("%d is not a palindrome number",num);
return0;
}
```

Check palindrome using recursion

```c
#include<stdio.h>
int check_palindrome(int num){
staticint reverse_num=0,rem;
if(num!=0){
    rem=num%10;
    reverse_num=reverse_num*10+rem;
    check_palindrome(num/10);
}
return reverse_num;
}
int main(){
int num, reverse_num;
  printf("Enter a number: ");
  scanf("%d",&num);
  reverse_num = check_palindrome(num);
if(num==reverse_num)
    printf("%d is a palindrome number",num);
else
    printf("%d is not a palindrome number",num);
return0;
}
```

C Program – Generating palindrome numbers in a given range

```c
#include<stdio.h>

int main()

{

int num, rem, reverse_num, temp, start,end;
   printf("Enter the lower limit: ");
   scanf("%d",&start);
   printf("Enter the upper limit: ");
   scanf("%d",&end);
   printf("Palindrome numbers between %d and %d are: ",start,end);
for(num=start;num<=end;num++){
    temp=num;
    reverse_num=0;
while(temp){
    rem=temp%10;
    temp=temp/10;
    reverse_num=reverse_num*10+rem;
}
if(num==reverse_num)
    printf("%d ",num);
}
return0;
}
```

C Program to check if number is even or odd
Using Modulus operator

```c
#include<stdio.h>
int main()
{
int num;
  printf("Enter an integer: ");
   scanf("%d",&num);
if( num%2==0)
    printf("%d is an even number", num);
else
    printf("%d is an odd number", num);

return0;
}
```

Using Bitwise operator

```c
#include<stdio.h>
int main()
{
int n;

    printf("Enter an integer: ");
    scanf("%d",&n);

if( n &1)
    printf("%d is an odd number", n);
else
    printf("%d is an even number", n);

return0;
}
```

Calculation of income tax for an employee

```c
#include <stdio.h>
#include <conio.h>
void main()
 {
 float income,tax;
 clrscr();
 printf("Enter Annual Income Amount :");
 scanf("%f",&income);
 if (income <= 250000)
  {
  printf("NO TAX");
  }
 if (income>250000 && income<=500000)
  {
  tax=income*5.0/100.0;
  printf("Tax = %10.2f",tax);
  }
 if (income>500000 && income<=1000000)
  {
  tax=income*20.0/100.0;
  printf("Tax = %10.2f",tax);
  }
 if (income>1000000)
  {
  tax=income*30.0/100.0;
  printf("Tax = %10.2f",tax);
  }
```

```
getch();
}
```

Displaying Multiplication Table

```c
#include <stdio.h>
#include <conio.h>
void main()
 {
 int k,n,m;
 clrscr();
 printf("Enter a number : ");
 scanf("%d",&n);
 printf("Multiplication Table of %d\n",n);
 for (k=1;k<=10;k++)
  {
  m=k*n;
  printf("%d",k);
  printf(" * ");
  printf("%d",n);
  printf(" = ");
  printf("%d",m);
  printf("\n");
  }
 getch();
 }
```

Program to display ASCII value of a character entered by user

```c
#include<stdio.h>
int main()
{
char ch;
    printf("Enter any character:");
    scanf("%c",&ch);
    printf("ASCII value of character %c is: %d", ch, ch);
return0;
}
```

C Program to find the Size of int, float, double and char

```c
#include<stdio.h>
int main()
{
    printf("Size of char: %ld byte\n",sizeof(char));
    printf("Size of int: %ld bytes\n",sizeof(int));
    printf("Size of float: %ld bytes\n",sizeof(float));
    printf("Size of double: %ld bytes",sizeof(double));
return0;
}
```

Program to check Vowel or Consonant

```c
#include<stdio.h>
int main()
{
char ch;
bool isVowel =false;

    printf("Enter an alphabet: ");
    scanf("%c",&ch);

if(ch=='a'||ch=='A'||ch=='e'||ch=='E'||ch=='i'||ch=='I'
                    ||ch=='o'||ch=='O'||ch=='u'||ch=='U')
{
        isVowel =true;

}
if(isVowel ==true)
     printf("%c is a Vowel", ch);
else
     printf("%c is a Consonant", ch);
return0;
}
```

C – If statement

```c
#include<stdio.h>
int main()
{
int x =20;
int y =22;
if(x<y)
{
    printf("Variable x is less than y");
}
return0;
}
```

If else statement

```c
#include<stdio.h>
int main()
{
int age;
   printf("Enter your age:");
   scanf("%d",&age);
if(age >=18)
{
        printf("You are eligible for voting");
}
else
{
        printf("You are not eligible for voting");
}
return0;
}
```

C Program to check Leap Year

```c
#include<stdio.h>
int main()
{
int y;

   printf("Enter year: ");
   scanf("%d",&y);

if(y %4==0)
{
          //Nested if else
if( y %100==0)
{
if( y %400==0)
          printf("%d is a Leap Year", y);
else
          printf("%d is not a Leap Year", y);
}
else
      printf("%d is a Leap Year", y );
}
else
    printf("%d is not a Leap Year", y);

return0;
}
```

Program to find sum of natural numbers using for loop

```c
#include<stdio.h>
int main()
{
int n, count, sum =0;

    printf("Enter the value of n(positive integer): ");
    scanf("%d",&n);

for(count=1; count <= n; count++)
{
    sum = sum + count;
}

    printf("Sum of first %d natural numbers is: %d",n, sum);

return0;
}
```

while loop in C programming

```c
#include<stdio.h>
int main()
{
int count=1;
while(count <=4)
{
        printf("%d ", count);
        count++;
}
return0;
}
```

C Program to convert uppercase string to lowercase string

```c
#include<stdio.h>
#include<string.h>
int main(){
char str[25];
int i;
   printf("Enter the string: ");
   scanf("%s",str);


for(i=0;i<=strlen(str);i++){
if(str[i]>=65&&str[i]<=90)
      str[i]=str[i]+32;
}
   printf("\nLower Case String is: %s",str);
return0;
}
```

C Program to convert lowercase string to uppercase string

```c
#include<stdio.h>
#include<string.h>
int main(){
char str[25];
int i;

  printf("Enter the string:");
  scanf("%s",str);

for(i=0;i<=strlen(str);i++){
if(str[i]>=97&&str[i]<=122)
    str[i]=str[i]-32;
}
  printf("\nUpper Case String is: %s",str);
return0;
  }
```

C Program – Sorting of a Set of Strings in Ascending alphabetical order

```c
#include<stdio.h>
#include<string.h>
int main(){
int i,j,count;
char str[25][25],temp[25];
    puts("How many strings u are going to enter?: ");
    scanf("%d",&count);

    puts("Enter Strings one by one: ");
for(i=0;i<=count;i++)
    gets(str[i]);
for(i=0;i<=count;i++)
for(j=i+1;j<=count;j++){
if(strcmp(str[i],str[j])>0){
        strcpy(temp,str[i]);
        strcpy(str[i],str[j]);
        strcpy(str[j],temp);
}
}
    printf("Order of Sorted Strings:");
for(i=0;i<=count;i++)
    puts(str[i]);

return0;
}
```

C Program – finding length of a String without using standard library function strlen

```c
#include<stdio.h>
int main()
{
char str[100],i;
   printf("Enter a string: \n");
   scanf("%s",str);

for(i=0; str[i]!='\0';++i);
    printf("\nLength of input string: %d",i);

return0;
}
```

Program for string concatenation

```c
#include<stdio.h>
int main()
{
char str1[50], str2[50], i, j;
    printf("\nEnter first string: ");
    scanf("%s",str1);
    printf("\nEnter second string: ");
    scanf("%s",str2);


for(i=0; str1[i]!='\0';++i);


for(j=0; str2[j]!='\0';++j,++i)
{
    str1[i]=str2[j];
}
    str1[i]='\0';
  printf("\n %s",str1);

return0;
}
```

C program to Reverse a String using recursion

```c
#include<stdio.h>
#include<string.h>
void reverse_string(char*,int,int);
int main()
{
char string_array[150];
    printf("Enter any string:");
    scanf("%s",&string_array);
    reverse_string(string_array,0, strlen(string_array)-1);
    printf("\nReversed String is: %s",string_array);
return0;
}
void reverse_string(char*x,int start,intend)
{
char ch;
if(start >=end)
return;
    ch =*(x+start);
*(x+start)=*(x+end);
*(x+end)= ch;
    reverse_string(x,++start,--end);
}
```

C Program to arrange numbers in ascending order

```c
#include<stdio.h>
void sort_numbers_ascending(int number[],int count)
{
int temp, i, j, k;
for(j =0; j < count;++j)
{
for(k = j +1; k < count;++k)
{
if(number[j]> number[k])
{
        temp = number[j];
        number[j]= number[k];
        number[k]= temp;
}
}
}
   printf("Numbers in ascending order:\n");
for(i =0; i < count;++i)
    printf("%d\n", number[i]);
}
void main()
{
int i, count, number[20];

   printf("How many numbers you are gonna enter:");
   scanf("%d",&count);
```

```c
    printf("\nEnter the numbers one by one:");

    for(i =0; i < count;++i)
        scanf("%d",&number[i]);

    sort_numbers_ascending(number, count);
}
```

C Program to find largest element of an Array

```c
#include<stdio.h>
int largest_element(int arr[],int num)
{
int i, max_element;
   max_element = arr[0];


for(i =1; i < num; i++)
if(arr[i]> max_element)
        max_element = arr[i];

return max_element;
}

int main()
{
int arr[]={1,24,145,20,8,-101,300};
int n =sizeof(arr)/sizeof(arr[0]);
   printf("Largest element of array is %d", largest_element(arr, n));
return0;
}
```

Sum of array elements using Recursion: Function calling itself

```c
#include<stdio.h>
int main()
{
int array[]={1,2,3,4,5,6,7};
int sum;
   sum = sum_array_elements(array,6);
   printf("\nSum of array elements is:%d",sum);
return0;
}
int sum_array_elements(int arr[],int n ){
if(n <0){
return0;
}else{
return arr[n]+ sum_array_elements(arr, n-1);
}
}
```

Sum of array elements using pointers

```c
#include<stdio.h>
int main()
{
int array[5];
int i,sum=0;
int*ptr;
    printf("\nEnter array elements (5 integer values):");
for(i=0;i<5;i++)
    scanf("%d",&array[i]);
  ptr = array;

for(i=0;i<5;i++)
{
    sum = sum +*ptr;
    ptr++;
}

  printf("\nThe sum is: %d",sum);
}
```

Program to find the size of an array

```c
#include<stdio.h>
int main()
{
double arr[]={11,22,33,44,55,66};
int n;


   n =sizeof(arr)/sizeof(arr[0]);
   printf("Size of the array is: %d\n", n);
return0;
}
```

C Program to Find the Largest of three numbers using Pointers

```c
#include<stdio.h>

int main()

{

int num1, num2, num3;

int*p1,*p2,*p3;

    printf("Enter First Number: ");

    scanf("%d",&num1);

    printf("Enter Second Number: ");

    scanf("%d",&num2);

    printf("Enter Third Number: ");

    scanf("%d",&num3);

    p1 =&num1;

    p2 =&num2;

    p3 =&num3;

if(*p1 >*p2)

{

        if(*p1 >*p3)

        {

                printf("%d is the largest number",*p1);

        }

        else

        {

                printf("%d is the largest number",*p3);

        }

}

else
```

```c
{
    if(*p2 >*p3)
    {
        printf("%d is the largest number",*p2);
    }
    else
    {
        printf("%d is the largest number",*p3);
    }
}
return0;
}
```

C Program to Count Vowels and Consonants in a String using Pointer

```c
#include<stdio.h>
int main()
{
char str[100];
char*p;
int  vCount=0,cCount=0;

   printf("Enter any string: ");
   fgets(str,100, stdin);
     p=str;
while(*p!='\0')
{
if(*p=='A'||*p=='E'||*p=='I'||*p=='O'||*p=='U'
                ||*p=='a'||*p=='e'||*p=='i'||*p=='o'||*p=='u')
      vCount++;
else
      cCount++;
    p++;
}

   printf("Number of Vowels in String: %d\n",vCount);
   printf("Number of Consonants in String: %d",cCount);
return0;
}
```

C Program to Print String using Pointer

```c
#include<stdio.h>
int main()
{
char str[100];
char*p;

    printf("Enter any string: ");
    fgets(str,100, stdin);
    p=str;
    printf("The input string is: ");
//'\0' signifies end of the string
while(*p!='\0')
        printf("%c",*p++);

return0;
    }
```

C Program to Swap two numbers using Pointers

```c
#include<stdio.h>
void swap(int*x,int*y)
{
int t;
    t  =*x;
*x  =*y;
*y  = t;
}

int main()
{
int num1,num2;

   printf("Enter value of num1: ");
   scanf("%d",&num1);
   printf("Enter value of num2: ");
   scanf("%d",&num2);
   printf("Before Swapping: num1 is: %d, num2 is:
%d\n",num1,num2);
   swap(&num1,&num2);
   printf("After  Swapping: num1 is: %d, num2 is:
%d\n",num1,num2);
return0;
}
```

C program to create, initialize and access a pointer variable

```c
#include<stdio.h>
int main()
{
char ch;
char*pCh;
    pCh =&ch;
    ch ='A';
    printf("Value of ch: %c\n",ch);
    printf("Address of ch: %p\n",&ch);
    printf("Value of ch: %c\n",*pCh);
    printf("Address of ch: %p",pCh);

return0;
}
```

C program to calculate and print the value of nPr

```c
#include<stdio.h>
void main()
{
int n, r, npr_var;
    printf("Enter the value of n:");
    scanf("%d",&n);
    printf("\nEnter the value of r:");
    scanf("%d",&r);
  npr_var = fact(n)/ fact(n - r);
    printf("\nThe value of P(%d,%d) is: %d",n,r,npr_var);
}
int fact(int num)
{
int k =1, i;
if(num ==0)
{
return(k);
}
else
{
for(i =1; i <= num; i++)
{
        k = k * i;
            }
}
return(k); }
```

C program to calculate and print the value of nCr

```c
#include<stdio.h>

int fact(int num);

void main()
{
int n, r, ncr_var;

    printf("Enter the value of n:");
    scanf("%d",&n);
    printf("\nEnter the value of r:");
    scanf("%d",&r);

    ncr_var = fact(n)/(fact(r)* fact(n - r));
    printf("\nThe value of C(%d,%d) is: %d",n,r,ncr_var);
}
int fact(int num)
{
int k =1, i;
// factorial of 0 is 1
if(num ==0)
{
return(k);
}
else
{
for(i =1; i <= num; i++)
```

```
    {
        k = k * i;
        }
}
return(k);
}
```

C Program to Multiply two Floating Point Numbers

```c
#include<stdio.h>
int main(){
float num1, num2, product;
    printf("Enter first Number: ");
    scanf("%f",&num1);
    printf("Enter second Number: ");
    scanf("%f",&num2);
    product = num1 * num2;
    printf("Product of entered numbers is:%.3f", product);
return0;
    }
```

Program to multiply two numbers using function

```c
#include<stdio.h>
float product(float a,float b){
return a*b;
}
int main()
{
float num1, num2, prod;
    printf("Enter first Number: ");
    scanf("%f",&num1);
    printf("Enter second Number: ");
    scanf("%f",&num2);
    prod  = product(num1, num2);
    printf("Product of entered numbers is:%.3f", prod);
return0;
}
```

Program to find Quotient and Remainder

```c
#include<stdio.h>
int main(){
int num1, num2, quot, rem;

  printf("Enter dividend: ");
  scanf("%d",&num1);

  printf("Enter divisor: ");
  scanf("%d",&num2);
  quot = num1 / num2;

  rem = num1 % num2;

  printf("Quotient is: %d\n", quot);
  printf("Remainder is: %d", rem);

return0;
  }
```

C Program to find the Average of two numbers

```c
#include<stdio.h>
int main()
{
int num1, num2;
float avg;

    printf("Enter first number: ");
    scanf("%d",&num1);
    printf("Enter second number: ");
    scanf("%d",&num2);
  avg=(float)(num1+num2)/2;
    printf("Average of %d and %d is: %.2f",num1,num2,avg);
return0;
}
```

Program to find the average using function

```c
#include<stdio.h>
float average(int a,int b){
return(float)(a+b)/2;
}
int main()
{
int num1, num2;
float avg;
   printf("Enter first number: ");
   scanf("%d",&num1);
   printf("Enter second number: ");
   scanf("%d",&num2);
   avg = average(num1, num2);
   printf("Average of %d and %d is: %.2f",num1,num2,avg);
return0;
}
```

Calculation of mean by using Array

```c
#include <stdio.h>
#include <conio.h>
void main()
 {
  int a[100], n,k,sum;
  float mean;
  printf("Enter total numbers : ");
  scanf("%d",&n);
  printf("Enter %d numbers :\n",n);
  sum=0;
  for (k=1;k<=n;k++)
   {
    scanf("%d",&a[k]);
    sum=sum+a[k];
   }
  mean=(float)sum/n;
  printf("\nThe given numbers are : ");
  for (k=1;k<=n;k++)
   {
    printf("%d ",a[k]);
   }
  printf("\n");
  printf("Mean : %10.2f",mean);
  getch();
 }
```

Counting Positive, Negative and Zero in an Array

```c
#include <stdio.h>
#include <conio.h>
void main()
 {
 int a[50];
 int n,k,pos,neg,zero;
 pos=0;
 neg=0;
 zero=0;
 clrscr();
 printf("Enter total numbers :");
 scanf("%d",&n);
 printf("Enter %d numbers :\n",n);
 for (k=1;k<=n;k++)
  {
   scanf("%d",&a[k]);
   if (a[k]>0) pos++;
   if (a[k]<0) neg++;
   if (a[k]==0) zero++;
  }
 printf("Positive numbers = %d\n",pos);
 printf("Negative numbers = %d\n",neg);
 printf("Zero numbers = %d",zero);
 getch();
 }
```

Program to convert binary to decimal

```c
#include<stdio.h>
#include<math.h>
int binaryToDecimal(long binarynum)
{
int decimalnum =0, temp =0, remainder;
while(binarynum!=0)
{
    remainder = binarynum %10;
    binarynum = binarynum /10;
    decimalnum = decimalnum + remainder*pow(2,temp);
    temp++;
}
return decimalnum;
}

int main()
{
long binarynum;
   printf("Enter a binary number: ");
   scanf("%ld",&binarynum);

   printf("Equivalent decimal number is: %d",
binaryToDecimal(binarynum));
return0;
}
```

Program to convert Decimal to Binary

```c
#include<stdio.h>
#include<math.h>

long decimalToBinary(int decimalnum)
{
long binarynum =0;
int rem, temp =1;

while(decimalnum!=0)
{
    rem = decimalnum%2;
    decimalnum = decimalnum /2;
    binarynum = binarynum + rem*temp;
    temp = temp *10;
}
return binarynum;
}

int main()
{
int decimalnum;
   printf("Enter a Decimal Number: ");
   scanf("%d",&decimalnum);
   printf("Equivalent Binary Number is: %ld",
decimalToBinary(decimalnum));
return0;
}
```

Program to convert decimal to octal

```c
#include<stdio.h>
#include<math.h>
int decimalToOctal(int decimalnum)
{
int octalnum =0, temp =1;

while(decimalnum !=0)
{
        octalnum = octalnum +(decimalnum %8)* temp;
        decimalnum = decimalnum /8;
    temp = temp *10;
}

return octalnum;
}
int main()
{
int decimalnum;

   printf("Enter a Decimal Number: ");
   scanf("%d",&decimalnum);

   printf("Equivalent Octal Number: %d",
decimalToOctal(decimalnum));
return0;}
```

Program to Convert Octal to Decimal

```c
#include<stdio.h>
#include<math.h>
long octalToDecimal(int octalnum)
{
int decimalnum =0, temp =0;

while(octalnum !=0)
{
    decimalnum = decimalnum +(octalnum%10)* pow(8,temp);
    temp++;
    octalnum = octalnum /10;
}

return decimalnum;
}
int main()
{
int octalnum;

   printf("Enter an octal number: ");
   scanf("%d",&octalnum);

   printf("Equivalent decimal number is: %ld",
octalToDecimal(octalnum));

return0;
}
```

Program to convert Binary to Octal

```c
#include<stdio.h>
#include<math.h>
int binaryToOctal(long binarynum)
{
int octalnum =0, decimalnum =0, i =0;
while(binarynum !=0)
{
    decimalnum = decimalnum +(binarynum%10)* pow(2,i);
    i++;
    binarynum = binarynum /10;
}
  i =1;
while(decimalnum !=0)
{
    octalnum = octalnum +(decimalnum %8)* i;
    decimalnum = decimalnum /8;
    i = i *10;
}
return octalnum;
}
int main()
{long binarynum;
   printf("Enter a binary number: ");
   scanf("%ld",&binarynum);
   printf("Equivalent octal value: %d", binaryToOctal(binarynum));
return0;}
```

Program to convert octal to binary

```c
#include<stdio.h>
#include<math.h>
long octalToBinary(int octalnum)
{
int decimalnum =0, i =0;
long binarynum =0;


while(octalnum !=0)
{
        decimalnum = decimalnum +(octalnum%10)* pow(8,i);
        i++;
        octalnum = octalnum /10;
}
   i =1
while(decimalnum !=0)
{
        binarynum = binarynum +(decimalnum %2)* i;
        decimalnum = decimalnum /2;
        i = i *10;
}
return binarynum;
}
int main()
{
int octalnum;
   printf("Enter an octal number: ");
```

```c
    scanf("%d",&octalnum);
    printf("Equivalent binary number is: %ld",
octalToBinary(octalnum));
return0; }
```

Program to calculate Area and Circumference based on user input

```c
#include<stdio.h>
int main()
{
int circle_radius;
float PI_VALUE=3.14, circle_area, circle_circumf;
    printf("\nEnter radius of circle: ");
    scanf("%d",&circle_radius);
    circle_area = PI_VALUE * circle_radius * circle_radius;
    printf("\nArea of circle is: %f",circle_area);
    circle_circumf =2* PI_VALUE * circle_radius;
    printf("\nCircumference of circle is: %f",circle_circumf);
return(0);
}
```

C Program to calculate Area of Equilatral triangle

```c
#include<stdio.h>
#include<math.h>
int main()
{
int triangle_side;
float triangle_area, temp_variable;
    printf("\nEnter the Side of the triangle:");
    scanf("%d",&triangle_side);
    temp_variable = sqrt(3)/4;
    triangle_area = temp_variable * triangle_side * triangle_side ;
    printf("\nArea of Equilateral Triangle is: %f",triangle_area);
return(0);
}
```

C Program to Print names of all Files present in a Directory

```c
#include<stdio.h>
#include<dirent.h>

int main(void)
{
    DIR *d;
    struct dirent *dir;
    d =opendir(".");
if(d)
{
while((dir =readdir(d))!= NULL)
{
printf("%s\n", dir->d_name);
}
closedir(d);
}
return(0);
}
```

Copying the contents of one file to another file

```c
#include <stdio.h>
#include <conio.h>
void main()
{
FILE *sfp,*dfp;
char file1[50],file2[50];
char ch;
clrscr();
printf("Enter the source filename : ");
gets(file1);
printf("Enter the new filename for copying : ");
gets(file2);
sfp=fopen(file1,"r");
dfp=fopen(file2,"w");
while (feof(sfp)==0)
 {
  ch=fgetc(sfp);
  fputc(ch,dfp);
 }
fclose(sfp);
fclose(dfp);
printf("The %s is copied into %s\n",file1,file2);
printf("The file content is \n");
dfp=fopen(file2,"r");
 while (feof(dfp)==0)
```

```c
    {
        ch=fgetc(dfp);
        printf("%c",ch);
    }
fclose(dfp);   getch(); }
```

Separating odd and even numbers in a file

```c
#include <stdio.h>
#include <conio.h>
void main()
 {
 FILE *nfp,*ofp,*efp;
 char file[50];
 int k,num;
 clrscr();
 printf("Enter the filename : ");
 gets(file);
 nfp=fopen(file,"r");
 ofp=fopen("odd.txt","w");
 efp=fopen("even.txt","w");
 while (1)
  {
   fscanf(nfp,"%d",&num);
   if feof(nfp) break;
   if (num%2==1)
   fprintf(ofp,"%d\n",num);
   else
   fprintf(efp,"%d\n",num);
  }
 fclose(nfp);
 fclose(ofp);
 fclose(efp);
 printf("The odd numbers are :\n");
```

```c
ofp=fopen("odd.txt","r");
while (1)
 {
  fscanf(ofp,"%d",&num);
  if feof(ofp) break;
  printf("%d\n",num);
 }
printf("The even numbers are :\n");
efp=fopen("even.txt","r");
while (1)
 {
  fscanf(efp,"%d",&num);
  if (feof(efp)) break;
  printf("%d\n",num);
 }
getch();
}
```

C Program to copy string using strcpy() Function

```c
#include<stdio.h>
#include<string.h>
int main()
{
    char mj[100];
   char aj[100];
printf("\n\nstrcpy(destination, source): is a system defined method
used to copy the source string into the destination.\n\n");
printf("\n\nEnter the string: ");
gets(aj);
strcpy(mj, aj);
printf("\n\nThe copied string is: %s\n\n", mj);
return0;
}
```

C Program to copy string without strcpy() function

```c
#include<stdio.h>
void stringCopy(char[], char[]);
int main()
{
    char aj[100], mj[100];
printf("\n\nEnter 1st string: ");
gets(aj);
stringCopy(aj, mj);
printf("\n\nThe copied string is: %s\n\n", mj);
return0;
}
void stringCopy(char a[], char b[])
{
    int i =0;
while(a[i]!='\0')
{
    b[i]= a[i];
    i++;
}

    b[i]=' \0';
}
```

How to use gets() function

```c
#include<stdio.h>

int main()
{
    char str[50];
gets(str);
printf("\n\nC Programming  %s\n\n\n", str);
return0;
}
```

Switch Case with break

```c
#include<stdio.h>
int main()
{
    char grade;
scanf("%c",&grade);
switch(grade)
{
     case 'A':
printf("Excellent\n");
break;
     case 'B':
printf("Keep it up!\n\n");
break;
     case 'C':
printf("Well done\n");
break;
     case 'D':
printf("You passed\n");
break;
     case 'F':
printf("Better luck next time\n");
break;
      default:
printf("Invalid grade\n");
}
printf("Your grade is %c\n",grade);
return0;}
```

Switch Case without break

```c
#include<stdio.h>
int main()
{
    char grade;
printf("Enter your grade:\n");
scanf("%c",&grade);
switch(grade)
{
    case 'A':
printf("Excellent\n");
    case 'B':
printf("\n\n\nKeep it up!\n\n");
    case 'C':
printf("\n\n\t\tCase C : Well done !\n\n");
    case 'D':
printf("\t\tCase D : Passed!\n\n");
    case 'F':
printf("\t\tCase E : Next time try\n\n\n");
    default:
printf("\t\tDefault Case : Invalid grade\n\n\n");
}
printf("Your grade is %c\n",grade);
return0;
}
```

Program to check if input character is a vowel using Switch Case

```c
#include<stdio.h>
int main()
{
    char ch;
printf("Input a Character :  ");
scanf("%c",&ch);
switch(ch)
{
        case 'a':
        case 'A':
        case 'e':
        case 'E':
        case 'i':
        case 'I':
        case 'o':
        case 'O':
        case 'u':
        case 'U':
printf("\n\n%c is a vowel.\n\n", ch);
break;
        default:
printf("%c is not a vowel.\n\n", ch);
}
return0;
}
```

Basic do while Loop Program

```c
#include<stdio.h>

int main()
{
    int i =10;
do
{
printf("i = %d\n",i);
    i = i-1;
}
while(i >0);

printf("\n\The value of i after exiting the loop is %d\n\n", i);
return0;
}
```

Swapping tow Numbers without using a Temporary Variable

```c
#include<stdio.h>
#include<conio.h>

void main()
{
    int x =10, y =15;
    x = x + y -(y = x);
printf("x = %d and y = %d",x,y);
getch();
}
```

Program to find Sum of Digits of a Number

```c
#include<stdio.h>

int main()
{
        int n, sum =0, c, remainder;
        scanf("%d",&n);
        while(n !=0)
        {
        remainder = n%10;
        sum += remainder;
        n = n/10;
        }
        printf("\n\nSum of the digits of the entered number is  =
%d\n\n", sum);
        return0;
}
```

Program to reverse a String

```c
#include<stdio.h>
#include<conio.h>
void main()
{
    int i, j, k;
    char str[100];
    char rev[100];
printf("Enter a string:\t");
scanf("%s", str);
printf("The original string is %s\n", str);
for(i =0; str[i]!='\0'; i++);
{
    k = i-1;
}
for(j =0; j <= i-1; j++)
{
    rev[j]= str[k];
    k--;
}
printf("The reverse string is %s\n", rev);
getch();
}
```

Program to find Armstrong Number between 1 to 500

```c
#include<stdio.h>
#include<math.h>
int main()
{
    int n,sum,i,t,a;
printf("\n\n\nThe Armstrong numbers in between 1 to 500 are :
\n\n\n");

for(i =1; i <=500; i++)
{
    t = i;
    sum =0;
while(t !=0)
{
        a = t%10;
        sum += a*a*a;
        t = t/10;
}

if(sum == i)
printf("\n\t\t\t%d", i);
}
return0;
}
```

Program to check whether a number is Armstrong Number

```c
#include<stdio.h>
#include<math.h>

int main()
{
    int n, sum =0, c, t, a;
printf("Enter a number:  ");
scanf("%d",&n);
    t = n;
while(n !=0)
{
    a = n%10;
    sum += a*a*a;
    n = n/10;
}

printf("\n\n\n\t\t\tsum = %d", sum);

if(sum == t)
printf("\n\n\t\t%d is an armstrong number\n", t);
else
printf("\n\n\t\t%d is not an armstrong number\n", t);
return0;
}
```

Program to find exponential without using pow() method

```c
#include<stdio.h>
int main()
{

   int n, exp, exp1;
   long long int value =1;

printf("Enter the number and its exponential:\n\n");
scanf("%d%d",&n,&exp);

   exp1 = exp;
while(exp-->0)
{
     value *= n;}
printf("\n\n %d^%d = %lld\n\n", n, exp1, value);
return0;
}
```

Program to insert an element in an Array

```c
#include<stdio.h>
int main()
{
    int array[100], position, c, n, value;
printf("\n\nEnter number of elements in array:");
scanf("%d",&n);
printf("\n\nEnter %d elements\n", n);
for(c =0; c < n; c++)
scanf("%d",&array[c]);
printf("\n\nEnter the location where you want to insert new element: ");
scanf("%d",&position);
printf("\n\nEnter the value to insert: ");
scanf("%d",&value);
for(c = n-1; c >= position-1; c--)
    array[c+1]= array[c];
  array[position -1]= value;
printf("\n\nResultant array is: ");
for(c =0; c <= n; c++)
printf("%d  ", array[c]);
return0;

}
```

Simple Program to remove Duplicate Element in an Array

```c
#include<stdio.h>
#include<conio.h>
void main()
{
    int a[20], i, j, k, n;
clrscr();
printf("\nEnter array size: ");
scanf("%d",&n);
printf("\nEnter %d array element: ", n);
for(i =0; i < n; i++)
{
scanf("%d",&a[i]);
}
printf("\nOriginal array is: ");
for(i =0; i < n; i++)
{
printf(" %d", a[i]);
}
printf("\nNew array is: ");
for(i =0; i < n; i++)
{
for(j = i+1; j < n;)
{
if(a[j]== a[i])
{
for(k = j; k < n; k++)
```

```c
		{
			a[k]= a[k+1];
		}
		n--;
	}
	else
	{
		j++;
	}
	}
	}

for(i =0; i < n; i++)
{
printf("%d ", a[i]);
}
getch();
}
```

Program to check whether a two dimensional array is a Sparse Matrix

```c
#include<stdio.h>
int main()
{
    int n, m, c, d, matrix[10][10];
    int counter =0;
printf("\nEnter the number of rows and columns of the matrix \n\n");
scanf("%d%d",&m,&n);
printf("\nEnter the %d elements of the matrix \n\n", m*n);
for(c =0; c < m; c++)
{
for(d =0; d < n; d++)
{
scanf("%d",&matrix[c][d]);
if(matrix[c][d]==0)
        counter++;
}
}
printf("\n\nThe entered matrix is: \n\n");
for(c =0; c < m; c++){
for(d =0; d < n; d++)
{
printf("%d\t", matrix[c][d]);
}
printf("\n");
}
```

```c
if(counter >(m*n)/2)
printf("\n\nThe entered matrix is a sparse matrix\n\n");
else
printf("\n\nThe entered matrix is not a sparse matrix\n\n");


return0;
}
```

Program to remove Duplicate Element in an Array

```c
#include<stdio.h>
#include<conio.h>
void main()
{
    int a[20], i, j, k, n;
clrscr();
printf("\nEnter array size: ");
scanf("%d",&n);
printf("\nEnter %d array element: ", n);
for(i =0; i < n; i++)
{
scanf("%d",&a[i]);
}
printf("\nOriginal array is: ");
for(i =0; i < n; i++)
{
printf(" %d", a[i]);
}
printf("\nNew array is: ");
for(i =0; i < n; i++)
{
for(j = i+1; j < n;)
{
if(a[j]== a[i])
{
```

```c
for(k = j; k < n; k++)
{
            a[k]= a[k+1];
}
        n--;
}
else
{
        j++;
}
}
}


for(i =0; i < n; i++)
{
printf("%d ", a[i]);
}
getch();
}
```

Program to find Deteminant of 2x2 Matrix

```c
#include<stdio.h>
int main()
{
    int a[2][2], i, j;
    long determinant;
printf("\n\nEnter the 4 elements of the array\n");
for(i =0; i <2; i++)
for(j =0; j <2; j++)
scanf("%d",&a[i][j]);
printf("\n\nThe entered matrix is: \n\n");
for(i =0; i <2; i++)
{
for(j =0; j <2; j++)
{
printf("%d\t", a[i][j]);
}
printf("\n");// to move to the next row
}
    determinant = a[0][0]*a[1][1]- a[1][0]*a[0][1];
printf("\n\nDterminant of 2x2 matrix is : %d - %d =  %d",
a[0][0]*a[1][1], a[1][0]*a[0][1], determinant);

return0;
}
```

Calculation of Employee payroll using Structure

```c
#include <stdio.h>
#include <conio.h>
void main()
 {
  struct payroll
   {
     char ename[30];
     float basic,da,hra,pf,esi;
     float gpay,dedu,npay;
   };
  struct payroll emp;
  clrscr();
  printf("Enter Employee Name :");
  gets(emp.ename);
  printf("Enter Basic Pay :");
  scanf("%f",&emp.basic);
  emp.da=emp.basic*60.0/100.0;
  emp.hra=emp.basic*20.0/100.0;
  emp.gpay=emp.basic + emp.da + emp.hra;
  emp.pf=emp.basic*12.5/100.0;
  emp.esi=emp.basic*2.0/100.0;
  emp.dedu=emp.pf+emp.esi;
  emp.npay = emp.gpay - emp.dedu;
  printf("\nEmployee Name .......... :   ");
  puts(emp.ename);
  printf("Basic Pay............... : %10.2f\n",emp.basic);
  printf("Dearness Allowance...... : %10.2f\n",emp.da);
```

```c
printf("House Rent Allowance.... : %10.2f\n",emp.hra);
printf("Gross Pay................ : %10.2f\n\n",emp.gpay);

printf("Provident Fund.......... : %10.2f\n",emp.pf);
printf("Employee State Insurance : %10.2f\n",emp.esi);
printf("Total Deductions........ : %10.2f\n\n",emp.dedu);

printf("Net Pay................. : %10.2f",emp.npay);
getch();
}
```

Basic C Program for Pointer to a Pointer

```c
#include<stdio.h>
int main()
{
    int var;
    int *ptr;
    int **pptr;
    var =50;
    ptr =&var;
    pptr =&ptr;
printf("\n\nValue of var = %d\n\n", var);
printf("\n\nValue available at *ptr = %d\n\n",*ptr);
printf("\n\nValue available at **pptr = %d\n\n",**pptr);
return0;
}
```

C Program to check lowercase using islower() Function

```c
#include<stdio.h>
#include<ctype.h>
int main()
{
    int var1 ='D';
    int var2 ='2';
    int var3 ='a';
    int var4 =' ';
printf("Range of ASCII values of lowercase character is 97 to
122\n\n");
if(islower(var1))
{
printf("\n var1 = |%c| is lowercase character\n", var1);
}
else
{
printf("\nvar1 =|%c| is not lowercase character\n", var1);
}

if(islower(var2))
{
printf("\n var2 = |%c| is lowercase character\n", var2);
}
else
{
printf("\nvar2 =|%c| is not lowercase character\n", var2);
```

```c
}

if(islower(var3))
{
printf("\n var3 = |%c| is lowercase character\n", var3);
}
else
{
printf("\nvar3 =|%c| is not lowercse character\n", var3);
}

if(islower(var4))
{
printf("\n var4 = |%c| is a lowercase character\n", var4);
}
else
{
printf("\nvar4 =|%c| is not a lowercase character\n", var4);
}

return0;
}
```

Program to check uppercase using isupper() Function

```c
#include<stdio.h>
#include<ctype.h>
int main()
{
    int var1 ='D';
    int var2 =65;
    int var3 ='a';
    int var4 =98;
printf("Range of ASCII values of upper-case characters is 65 to
90\n\n");
if(isupper(var1))
{
printf("\n var1 = |%c| is a upper-case character\n", var1);
}
else
{
printf("\n var1 =|%c| is not a upper-case character\n", var1);
}


if(isupper(var2))
{
printf("\n var2 = |%c| is a upper-case character\n", var2);
}
else
{
```

```c
        printf("\n var2 =|%c| is not a upper-case character\n", var2);
    }
    return0;
}
```

**C Program to covert character to lowercase using tolower()
Function**

```c
#include<stdio.h>
#include<ctype.h>
int main()
{
printf("For example, ASCII value of a = %d and that of A =
%d.\n\n\n ",'a','A');
printf("\n\nThe lowercase equivalent of letter 'A' is '%c' ",'A'+32);
    int aj =0;
    char mj[]=" \n\n\n\n\"KEEP LEARNING, AS WHAT YOU
KNOW WILL NEVER BE ENOUGH!\"\n\n";

while(mj[aj]){
putchar(tolower(mj[aj]));
    aj++;
}
return0;
}
```

C Program to convert character(s) to uppercase using the toupper() Function

```c
include<stdio.h>
#include<ctype.h>
int main()
{
printf("\n\nThe uppercase equivalent of letter 'a' is %c.\n\n ",'a'-32);
    int aj =0;
    char mj[]=" \n\nKeep learning, as what you know will never be enough!\n\n";
while(mj[aj])
{
putchar(toupper(mj[aj]));
    aj++;
}
return0;
}
```

C Program to check if character is alphabet using isalpha()
Function

```c
#include<stdio.h>
#include<ctype.h>
int main()
{
    int var1 ='D';
  int var2 ='2';
  int var3 ='a';
  int var4 =' ';
if(isalpha(var1))
{
printf("\n var1 = |%c| is alphabet\n", var1);
}
else
{
printf("\n var1 =|%c| is not alphabet\n", var1);
}

if(isalpha(var2))
{
printf("\n var2 = |%c| is alphabet\n", var2);
}
else
{
printf("\n var2 =|%c| is not alphabet\n", var2);
```

```c
	}

	if(isalpha(var3))
	{
	printf("\n var3 = |%c| is alphabet\n", var3);
	}
	else
	{
	printf("\n var3 =|%c| is not alphabet\n", var3);
	}

	return0;
	}
```

**C Program to check if character is alphabet using isalpha()
Function**

```c
#include<stdio.h>
#include<ctype.h>
int main()
{
    int var1 ='D';
    int var2 ='2';
    int var3 ='a';
    int var4 =' ';
if(isalpha(var1))
{
printf("\n var1 = |%c| is alphabet\n", var1);
}
else
{
printf("\n var1 =|%c| is not alphabet\n", var1);
}
if(isalpha(var2))
{
printf("\n var2 = |%c| is alphabet\n", var2);
}
else
{
printf("\n var2 =|%c| is not alphabet\n", var2);
}return0;}
```

C Program to check if character string is alphanumeric using isalnum() Function

```c
#include<stdio.h>
#include<ctype.h>
int main()
{
    int var1 ='d';
    int var2 ='2';
    int var3 ='%';
    int var4 =' ';
if(isalnum(var1))
{
printf("\n var1 = |%c| is alphanumeric\n", var1);
}
else
{
printf("\nvar1 =|%c| is not alphanumeric\n", var1);
}

if(isalnum(var2))
{
printf("\n var2 = |%c| is alphanumeric\n", var2);
}
else
{
printf("\nvar2 =|%c| is not alphanumeric\n", var2);
}
return0;}
```

C program to merge two files

```c
#include <stdio.h>
#include <stdlib.h>
int main()
{
  FILE *fs1, *fs2, *ft;
char ch, file1[20], file2[20], file3[20];
  printf("Enter name of first file\n");
  gets(file1);
  printf("Enter name of second file\n");
  gets(file2);
  printf("Enter name of file which will store contents of the two
files\n");
  gets(file3);
  fs1 = fopen(file1, "r");
  fs2 = fopen(file2, "r");
  if (fs1 == NULL || fs2 == NULL)
  {
    perror("Error ");
    printf("Press any key to exit...\n");
    exit(EXIT_FAILURE);
  }
  ft = fopen(file3, "w");
  if (ft == NULL)
  {
    perror("Error ");
    printf("Press any key to exit...\n");
```

```c
        exit(EXIT_FAILURE);
    }
  while ((ch = fgetc(fs1)) != EOF)
    fputc(ch,ft);
 while ((ch = fgetc(fs2)) != EOF)
    fputc(ch,ft);
  printf("The two files were merged into %s file successfully.\n",
file3);
  fclose(fs1);
  fclose(fs2);
  fclose(ft);
  return 0;
 }
```

C program to delete a file

```c
#include <stdio.h>
int main()
{
  int status;
  char file_name[25];
  printf("Enter name of a file you wish to delete\n");
  gets(file_name);
  status = remove(file_name);
  if (status == 0)
    printf("%s file deleted successfully.\n", file_name);
  else
  {
    printf("Unable to delete the file\n");
  }
  return 0;
}
```

C program to generate random numbers

```c
#include <stdio.h>
#include <stdlib.h>
int main() {
  int c, n;
  printf("Ten random numbers in [1,100]\n");
  for (c = 1; c <= 10; c++) {
    n = rand() % 100 + 1;
    printf("%d\n", n);
  }
  return 0;
}
```

C program to print date

```c
#include <stdio.h>
#include <conio.h>
#include <dos.h>
int main()
{
   struct date d;
   getdate(&d);
   printf("Current system date: %d/%d/%d", d.da_day, d.da_mon,
d.da_year);
   getch();
   return 0;
}
```

C program to get IP address

```c
#include<stdlib.h>
int main()
{
  system("C:\\Windows\\System32\\ipconfig");


  return 0;
}
```

C program to shut down or turn off computer

```c
#include <stdio.h>
#include <stdlib.h>

int main()
{
  system("C:\\WINDOWS\\System32\\shutdown /s");

  return 0;
}
```

C program for Windows XP

```c
#include <stdio.h>
#include <stdlib.h>
int main()
{
    char ch;
    printf("Do you want to shutdown your computer now (y/n)\n");
    scanf("%c", &ch);
    if (ch == 'y' || ch == 'Y')
        system("C:\\WINDOWS\\System32\\shutdown -s");
    return 0;
}
```

C program to merge two arrays

```c
#include <stdio.h>
void merge(int [], int, int [], int, int []);
int main() {
  int a[100], b[100], m, n, c, sorted[200];
  printf("Input number of elements in first array\n");
  scanf("%d", &m);
  printf("Input %d integers\n", m);
  for (c = 0; c < m; c++) {
    scanf("%d", &a[c]);
  }
  printf("Input number of elements in second array\n");
  scanf("%d", &n);
  printf("Input %d integers\n", n);
  for (c = 0; c < n; c++) {
    scanf("%d", &b[c]);
  }
  merge(a, m, b, n, sorted);
  printf("Sorted array:\n");
  for (c = 0; c < m + n; c++) {
    printf("%d\n", sorted[c]);
  }
  return 0;
}
void merge(int a[], int m, int b[], int n, int sorted[]) {
  int i, j, k;
```

```c
j = k = 0;
for (i = 0; i < m + n;) {
  if (j < m && k < n) {
    if (a[j] < b[k]) {
      sorted[i] = a[j];
      j++;
    }
    else {
      sorted[i] = b[k];
      k++;
    }
    i++;
  }
  else if (j == m) {
    for (; i < m + n;) {
      sorted[i] = b[k];
      k++;
      i++;
    }
  }
  else {
    for (; i < m + n;) {
      sorted[i] = a[j];
      j++;
      i++;
    } }
  }
}
```

C program to print Floyd's triangle

```c
#include <stdio.h>
int main()
{
 int n, i,  c, a = 1;
 scanf("%d", &n);
  for (i = 1; i <= n; i++)
  {
   for (c = 1; c <= i; c++)
   {
    printf("%d ",a);
    a++;
   }
   printf("\n");
  }
  return 0;
}
```

C program to print Floyd's triangle using recursion

```c
#include <stdio.h>

void print_floyd(int);

int main()
{
  int n;
  scanf("%d", &n);

  print_floyd(n);

  return 0;
}

void print_floyd(int n) {
  static int row = 1, c = 1;
  int d;
  if (n <= 0)
    return;

  for (d = 1; d <= row; ++d)
    printf("%d ", c++);

  printf("\n");
  row++;
  print_floyd(--n);
}
```